Been There!
FRANCE

Annabel Savery

Facts about France

Population: 64 million

Capital city: Paris

Currency: Euro (€)

Main language: French

Rivers: Seine, Rhône, Loire, Saône

Area (mainland France): 547,030 square kilometres (211,209 square miles)

 An Appleseed Editions book

Paperback edition 2014

First published in 2011 by Franklin Watts
338 Euston Road, London NW1 3BH

Franklin Watts Australia
Level 17/207 Kent St, Sydney, NSW 2000

© 2011 Appleseed Editions

Created by Appleseed Editions Ltd,
Well House, Friars Hill, Guestling, East Sussex TN35 4ET

Planning and production by Discovery Books Limited
www.discoverybooks.net
Designed by Ian Winton
Edited by Annabel Savery
Map artwork by Stefan Chabluk

ISBN 978 1 4451 3287 7

Dewey Classification: 944'.084

A CIP catalogue for this book is available from the British Library.

Picture credits: Alamy: title & p18 (G P Bowater), p12 top (Peter Bowater), p21 (Danita Delimont); Corbis: p10 (The Gallery Collection), p11 top (Marc Deville), p26 (Doug Pearson); Discovery Picture Library: p13 (Chris Fairclough), p20 (Chris Fairclough); Eurotunnel: p28 (Turpin Philippe); Getty Images: p6 (Frederic Cirou), p9 top (Tom Bonaventure), p15 top (Daniel Mihailescu), p19 (Michael Busselle / Robert Harding), p22 (medioimages / photodisc), p25 top (FGP Intl), p25 bottom (DEA PICTURE LIBRARY); Istockphoto: p27 top; Shutterstock: p2 (Neo Edmund), p5 top & p30, p5 bottom (Amy Nichole Harris), p7 top, p7 bottom & p31, p8 (Stephen Finn), p9 bottom, p11 bottom (Marc Ragen), p12 bottom, p14, p15 bottom, pp16-17 (Boussac Marie Therese), p23 (Kitaeva Tatiana), p24, p27 bottom, p29.

Cover photos: Shutterstock: main (Angelina Dimitrova), left (imantsu), right (Marcel Jancovic).

Printed in Singapore.

Franklin Watts is a division of Hachette Children's Books, an Hachette UK company.
www.hachette.co.uk

Contents

Off to France!

We are going on holiday to France. France is a country in the continent of Europe.

France is divided into 26 parts called regions. Some of these regions are overseas. They are called **colonies**.

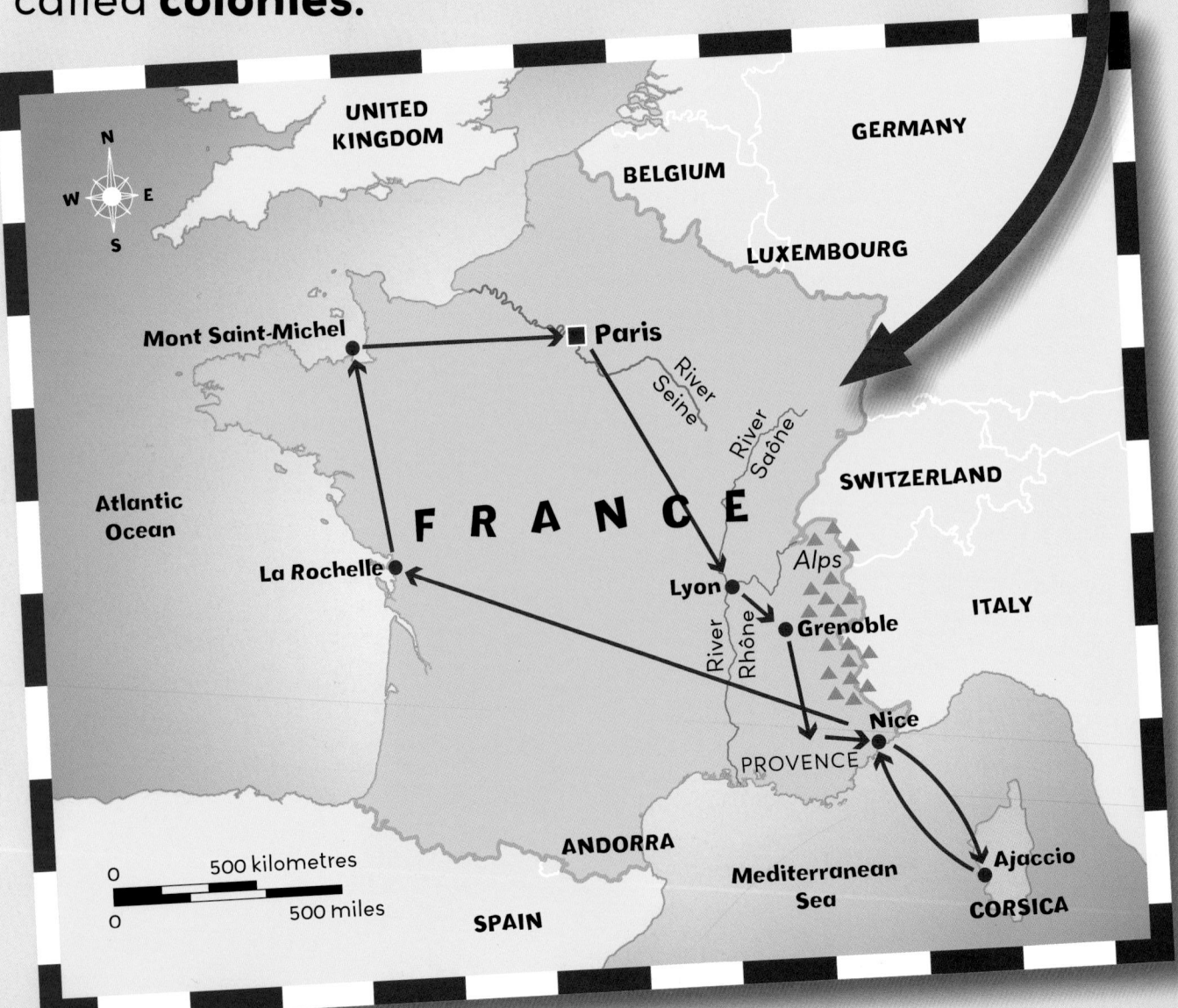

N W E S

UNITED KINGDOM

GERMANY

BELGIUM

LUXEMBOURG

Mont Saint-Michel

Paris

River Seine

River Saône

SWITZERLAND

Atlantic Ocean

F R A N C E

Alps

ITALY

La Rochelle

Lyon

River Rhône

Grenoble

Nice

PROVENCE

ANDORRA

Mediterranean Sea

Ajaccio

CORSICA

SPAIN

0 500 kilometres

0 500 miles

France can be both hot and cold, so I am packing lots of different clothes. Usually the weather is hotter in the south-east of the country, near the Mediterranean Sea.

Towards the north of the country it is often cooler.

Eiffel Tower

Here are some things I know about France...

- France is famous for foods, such as croissants, snails and cheese.
- The Eiffel Tower (left) is a famous landmark. It is in France's capital city, Paris.
- Many famous artists and writers came from France. Their work is still known today.

On our trip I'm going to find out lots more!

Arriving in Paris

We arrive in Paris in the early morning. A taxi takes us from the airport to our hotel.

The roads in the city are busy. Many drivers are beeping their horns.

Everyone is rushing around. Paris is the biggest city in Europe. Over 10 million people live here.

For breakfast we have bowls of hot chocolate, and croissants that are sweet and buttery. We dip the croissants in the hot chocolate. Yum!

In the afternoon we climb the Eiffel Tower. It is a very long way up and my legs get very tired. The view is amazing. We can see the whole of Paris.

Did you know that the Eiffel Tower is 324 metres (1,062 feet) tall? There are 1,653 steps to get to the top.

Exploring Paris

Today we are going to see more sights in Paris.

Our first stop is the *Arc de Triomphe*. This is a big stone archway. It is a **monument** to remember the people who have fought in wars for France.

The River Seine flows through the middle of Paris. At one place it splits in two, leaving an island in the middle. This is the *Isle de la Cité*. It is one of the oldest parts of Paris.

Notre-Dame de Paris

We cross over a bridge onto the island. Here there is a big cathedral called *Notre-Dame de Paris*. Inside it is cool and quiet. The windows are made of **stained glass**. They are very colourful.

In the afternoon we go to *La Defense*. This is the main business area and very modern. One building is shaped like a big, square arch.

The Palace of Versailles

I am very excited about visiting the Palace of Versailles. French kings and queens lived here a long time ago. The palace is south-west of Paris. We travel there on a coach.

The palace was built by a king called Louis XIV. He was a great king. XIV stands for fourteenth.

Louis XIV was known as the Sun King. He reigned for 72 years. Ceremonies were held when he got up and went to bed.

My favourite room is the Hall of Mirrors or *La Grande Galerie*. It is beautiful. There are mirrors on the walls and glass chandeliers hanging from the ceiling.

We walk around the lovely gardens too. There are many statues and beautiful fountains.

Whizzing to Lyon

Next, we are going to visit Lyon. We are going to travel on the TGV. This stands for *Train à Grande Vitesse*, which means 'high-speed train'.

Before we leave we buy a picnic lunch to eat on the train. We buy a long loaf of bread called a baguette, some cheese, a salami and lots of fruit.

We buy cheese called 'brie'. The outside is white and hard. The middle is creamy and gooey.

We travel out of Paris into open fields and woods. We pass through towns and see lots of villages. We cross rivers on big bridges and go through dark tunnels.

The train goes very quickly and it only takes two hours to travel the 512 kilometres (318 miles) to Lyon.

Old and new

There is a lot to see in Lyon. There are two rivers, the Saône and the Rhône.

There is an old part of town and a modern one. The main square is in the middle.

It is very busy in Lyon because there is a football match on. Lyon has one of the best football teams in

France. It is called *Olympique Lyonnaise*.

Other sports are popular in France too. The *Tour de France* is a bicycle race that is held in July every year. The course takes three weeks to complete and more than 100 cyclists take part.

Every December Lyon has the *Festival des Lumières* or Festival of Lights. All the buildings and monuments are decorated with bright, colourful lights.

In the Alps

Today we are going to Grenoble. This is a town near the Alps.

The Alps are a range of mountains. They are on the border of France, Switzerland and Italy. France has seven mountain ranges altogether.

From Grenoble we take a bus up into the mountains. The road is very steep. When I look out of the window I can see a long way down.

We go for a walk in the mountains. It is sunny and the mountains look very green. Dad says that in the winter there is snow everywhere and you can ski and snowboard here.

Did you know that the highest peak in the Alps is Mont Blanc? Mont Blanc is in France. It is 4,810 metres (15,781 feet) tall.

In Provence

From Grenoble we travel south through a region called Provence. It is very colourful here.

The land is divided up into fields. Some fields are green, some are yellow, and some are bright purple. The purple fields are lavender. The yellow fields are full of sunflowers.

Farming is a very important **industry** in France. Half of the land in France is used for farming.

We are going to stay in a farm cottage. The farm has a large **vineyard**.

Vineyards are areas where grapes are grown. These grapes are used to make wine. France sells a lot of wine to other countries.

The farmer and his wife speak Provençale. This is a local language that is spoken in this region. Luckily, they speak French and some English too.

Making friends

The farmer has two children. Luc is eleven. His sister Marie is eight. They don't speak much English and it is funny trying to talk to them.

They show me around the farm. They have some cows and a pig. Luc says he likes to help with the animals when he's not at school.

Marie says she likes school as she has lots of friends. But she doesn't like getting up early. Her school starts at eight o'clock. She and Luc both have to go to school on Saturday mornings too.

I'd like to go to school in France. Lots of French children go home for lunch and they don't have school on Wednesday afternoons.

The blue coast

Nice (pronounced Nees) is our next stop.
It is a big city on the south coast.

This part of the coast is called the *Cote d'Azur*,
this means the 'blue coast'. The sea is the
Mediterranean. Houses here are painted
bright colours, such as pink and blue. Some
are white with red roofs.

It is very warm in Nice and we spend a day playing by the sea. The beach is long and pebbly.

In the evening we eat in a restaurant by the beach. We share a seafood platter and *frites*. There are lots of different things on the platter. There's crab, big **langoustines**, clams, mussels and even octopus!

The waiter tells us that the seafood was caught the same day. It is very fresh and tasty.

A ferry to Corsica

From Nice we get on a ferry to Corsica. This is an island in the Mediterranean Sea. The journey will take six hours.

We are going to land at Ajaccio. This is a port on the west coast of the island. There are lots of yachts and fishing boats. Along the streets nearby there are palm trees.

Further inland, there are high mountains. These are covered with snow for a lot of the year.

Dad says that Ajaccio is quite famous because the Emperor Napoleon Bonaparte was born here. We visit a museum about him. I think he was a very powerful man.

Dad takes us to see some stone **menhirs**. These are stone statues. They were made by people who lived here thousands of years ago. After two days on the island we catch the ferry back to Nice.

La Rochelle

When we leave Nice we have a long drive to La Rochelle. This is a town on the west coast of France, by the Atlantic Ocean.

First, we look around the harbour. Dad says this used to be a very important place for buying and selling goods with other countries.

Mum has bought a French game called *pétanque*. We play on the beach. One person throws a small coloured ball, this is called the 'jack'.

Then we have to throw heavier balls and try and get them as close as possible to the jack. It is lots of fun.

For dinner I try eating snails! They are chewy and garlicky.

Mont Saint-Michel

It takes a long time to drive to the North coast. The sea at the north coast of France is called *La Manche*, this means 'the sleeve'. It is also called the English Channel. A tunnel goes under the sea to England.

Tunnel entrance

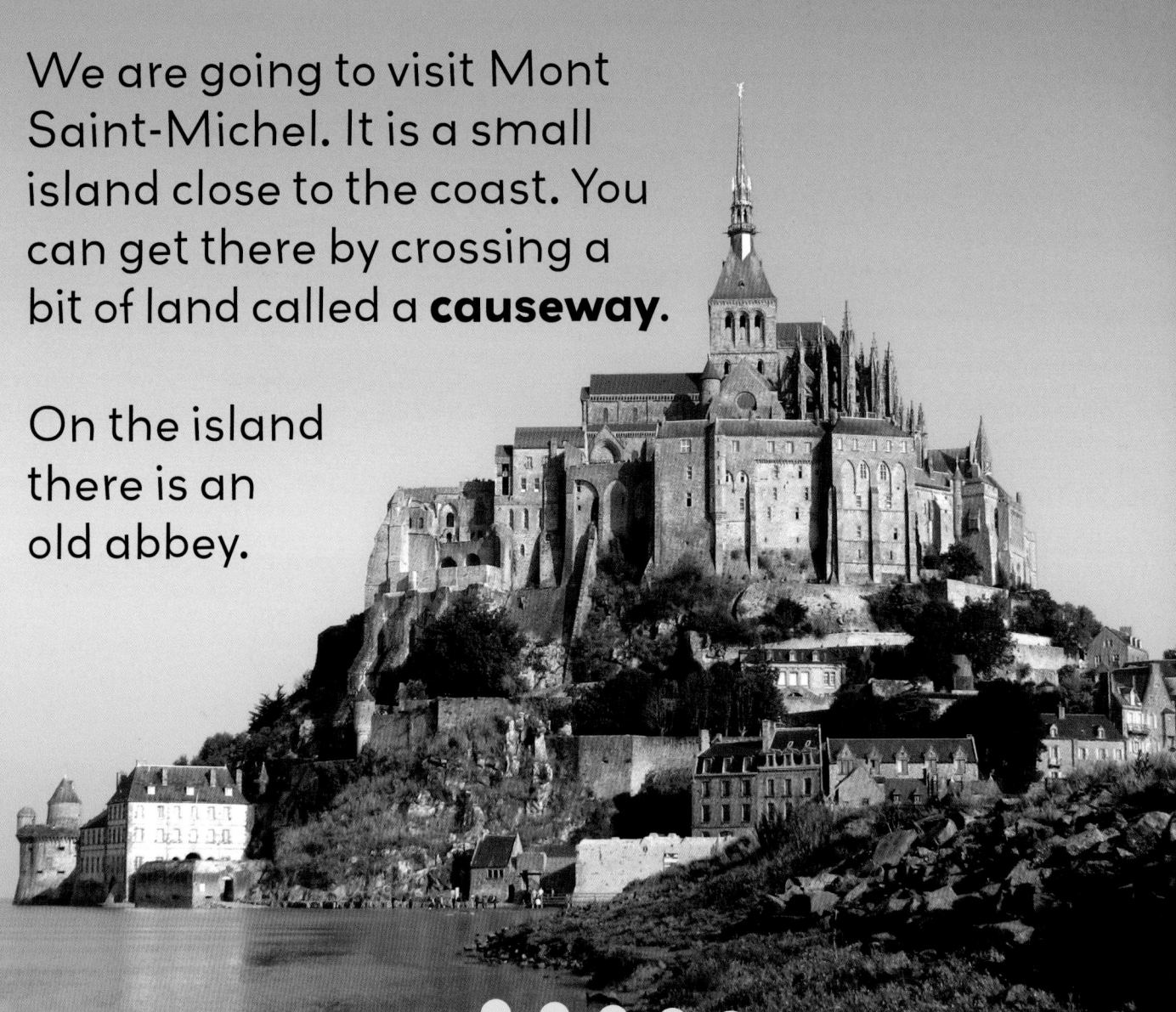

We are going to visit Mont Saint-Michel. It is a small island close to the coast. You can get there by crossing a bit of land called a **causeway**.

On the island there is an old abbey.

After looking at the abbey it is time to go home. We have to pack our bags and catch the train back to Paris.

The abbey is the oldest thing on the island. It was built first and then the town grew around it. At one time it was used as a prison.

My first words in French

Bonjour (*say* **Boh(n)zhoor**)   Hello

Au revoir (*say* **Oh rvwahr**)   Goodbye

Comment ça va?
(*say* **Kommon sa va?**)   How are you?

Ça va bien, merci.
(*say* **Sa va bian mehrsee**)   I'm fine, thank you.

Comment t'appelle-tu?
(*say* **Kommon tappel too?**)   What is your name?

Je m'appelle Dylan.
(*say* **Zhe mappel Dylan**)   My name is Dylan.

Counting 1-10

1 **un**   2 **deux**   3 **trois**   4 **quatre**

5 **cinq**   6 **six**   7 **sept**   8 **huit**

9 **neuf**

10 **dix**

Words to remember

causeway a raised road across low, wet ground

chandelier a large hanging light with many branches for light bulbs or candles

colony a country that is governed by another country

industry the people and processes involved in producing a particular thing

langoustine a type of large prawn

menhir a large stone that is placed on end; it might be decorated by carvings

monument something that is built in memory of a person or event

stained glass glass that has been coloured

vineyard an area of land where grapes are grown for making wine

Index

Learning more about France

Books

France (Country Insights) Teresa Fisher, Wayland, 2008.
France (Facts About Countries) C Tidmarsh, Franklin Watts, 2005.
France (Find Out About) Duncan Crosbie, Franklin Watts, 2006.
France (Looking at Countries) Jillian Powell, Franklin Watts, 2006.
France (My Holiday in) Susie Brooks, Wayland, 2008.

Websites

National Geographic Kids, People and places
http://kids.nationalgeographic.com/places/find/france
Geography for kids, Geography online and Geography games
http://www.kidsgeo.com/index.php
SuperKids Geography directory, lots of sites to help with geography learning.
http://www.super-kids.com/geography.html